American Indians in the 1800s

Right and Resistance

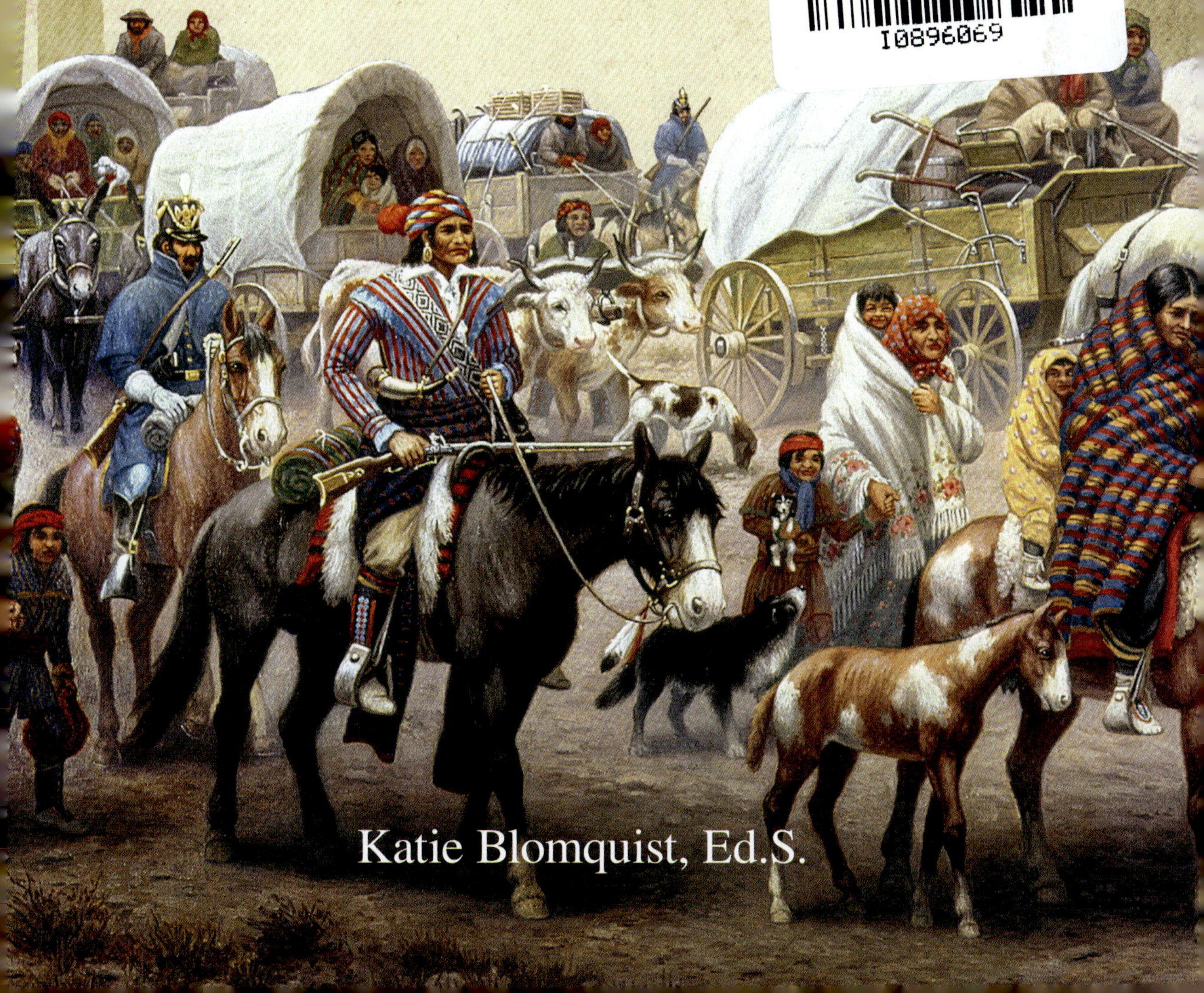

Katie Blomquist, Ed.S.

Consultants

Vanessa Ann Gunther, Ph.D.
Department of History
Chapman University

Nicholas Baker, Ed.D.
Supervisor of Curriculum and Instruction
Colonial School District, DE

Katie Blomquist, Ed.S.
Fairfax County Public Schools

Publishing Credits

Rachelle Cracchiolo, M.S.Ed., *Publisher*
Conni Medina, M.A.Ed., *Managing Editor*
Emily R. Smith, M.A.Ed., *Series Developer*
Diana Kenney, M.A.Ed., NBCT, *Content Director*
Courtney Patterson, *Senior Graphic Designer*
Lynette Ordoñez, *Editor*

Image Credits: Cover and pp. 1, 11 (top) Granger, NYC; pp. 2, 6, 9, back cover North Wind Picture Archives; p. 4 LOC [LC-DIG-pga-04158]; p. 5 (middle) LOC [gm72002042], (bottom) Architect of the Capitol; p. 7 (left) NARA [299800], (middle) NARA [12013254], (right) NARA [12013260]; p. 8 (left) LOC [LC-DIG-pga-02501], (right) NARA [5682743]; p. 10 LOC [LC-DIG-pga-07513]; p. 11 (middle) NARA [6860606], (bottom) NARA [2127291]; p. 12 Bridgeman Images; p. 13 Peter Newark American Pictures/Bridgeman Images; p. 14 LOC [LC-DIG-pga-07732]; pp. 14-15 LOC [LC-USZ62-130184]; p. 15 (top) LOC [LC-USZ62-91032], (bottom) NARA [299803]; p. 16 LOC [LC-DIG-cwpbh-03216]; p. 17 (top) GraphicaArtis/Bridgeman Images, (bottom) Chicago History Museum, USA/Bridgeman Images; p. 18 (top) Smithsonian Institution, Washington DC, USA/Bridgeman Images, (bottom) Look and Learn/Bridgeman Images; p. 20 (top)Look and Learn/Illustrated Papers Collection/Bridgeman Images, (bottom) Peter Newark American Pictures/ Bridgeman Images; p. 21 Sarin Images/Granger, NYC; p. 22 LOC [LC-DIG-ppmsc-02512]; p. 23 NARA [292877]; p. 24 Kevin Fleming/Corbis/VCG/Getty Images; p. 25 (top) Danita Delimont/Getty Images, (bottom) Omniphoto/UIG/ Bridgeman Images; p. 26 NARA [24068520]; p. 27 (top) Hemis/Alamy Stock Photo, (bottom) Cvandyke/Shutterstock.com; p. 28 Danita Delimont/Alamy Stock Photo; p. 29 Alvis Upitis/Newscom; p. 31 Chicago History Museum, USA/Bridgeman Images; p. 32 NARA [5682743]; all other images from iStock and/or Shutterstock.

Library of Congress Cataloging-in-Publication Data

Names: Blomquist, Katie, author.
Title: American Indians in the 1800s : right and resistance / Katie Blomquist.
Description: Huntington Beach, CA : Teacher Created Materials, [2017] | Includes index. | Audience: Grades 4-6.
Identifiers: LCCN 2016034143 (print) | LCCN 2016047978 (ebook) | ISBN 9781493837991 (pbk.) | ISBN 9781480757646 (eBook)
Subjects: LCSH: Indians of North America--History--19th century--Juvenile literature. | Indians of North America--Government relations--Juvenile literature. | Indians, Treatment of--North America--Juvenile literature.
|
Indian Removal, 1813-1903--Juvenile literature. | Indians of North America--Wars--1866-1895--Juvenile literature.
Classification: LCC E77.4 .B56 2017 (print) | LCC E77.4 (ebook) | DDC 323.1197--dc23
LC record available at https://lccn.loc.gov/2016034143

Teacher Created Materials
5301 Oceanus Drive
Huntington Beach, CA 92649-1030
http://www.tcmpub.com

ISBN 978-1-4938-3799-1

Printed by: 590835
Printed in: China

Table of Contents

The Nation Moves Westward 4

Removal 6

Resistance 12

Resilience 22

Looking Ahead 26

Remember It! 28

Glossary 30

Index 31

Your Turn! 32

The Nation Moves Westward

The evil, Sir, is enormous; the inevitable suffering incalculable… Nations of dependent Indians, against their will, under color of law, are driven from their homes into the wilderness…. Our friends will view this measure with sorrow, and our enemies alone with joy. And we ourselves, Sir, when the interests and passions of the day are past, shall look back upon it, I fear, with self-reproach, and a regret as bitter as ***unavailing****.*

—Edward Everett

In 1830, Congressman Everett spoke out against the forced removal of American Indians from their homes. Sadly, his view was not shared by all.

In the 19th century, the United States wanted to expand its borders. Many Americans felt that their nation should stretch from ocean to ocean. Settlers flocked to the West. Yet, they gave little thought to the plight of American Indians. They removed tribe after tribe from their **native** lands.

Tribes struggled to survive. More than 100,000 American Indians lost their homes. And, the death toll from forced removals reached into the thousands. Their story is marked by hardship. Yet, it also shows how the people were able to adapt and **endure** against all odds.

Edward Everett

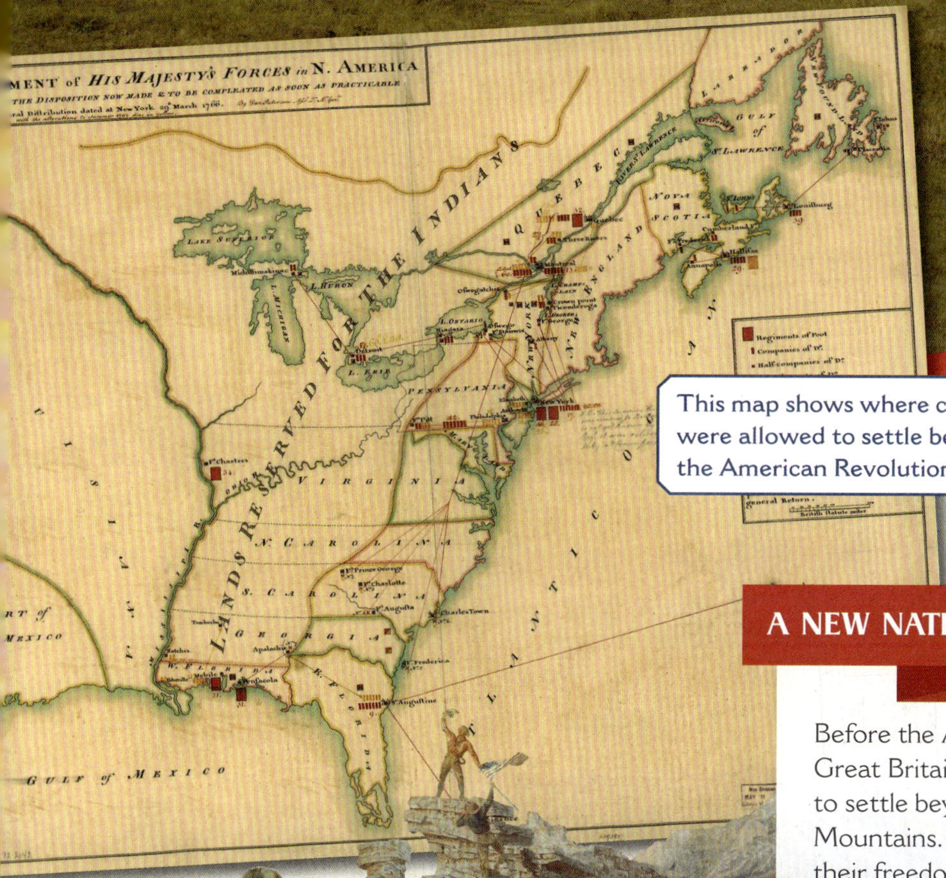

This map shows where colonists were allowed to settle before the American Revolution.

A NEW NATION

Before the American Revolution, Great Britain did not allow colonists to settle beyond the Appalachian Mountains. Once Americans won their freedom, they set their sights on the **frontier**.

Removal

American Indians and white settlers had clashed often since Europeans began settling in North America. White settlers took tribal land, and tribes fought to defend it. But, in the late 1700s, the United States took land with new force.

Dutch settlers sign a treaty with Mohawk Indians in the 1640s.

Broken Promises

The United States began making **treaties** with tribes. Treaties are solemn agreements between countries. They help nations live side by side in peace. Tribes made treaties with each other long before white settlers came to their lands. American Indian tribes signed more than 370 treaties with the United States. The first was signed in 1778.

Sometimes, these treaties were written in a confusing way. Not all tribes understood the terms of their treaties. In some cases, this allowed the U.S. government to take their land. The United States often violated treaties with tribes, too. Even when the United States agreed to stay off tribal land, they broke these promises again and again as white settlers moved west. Many tribes felt betrayed. They lost millions of acres of land and grew angry. In 1830, a new law forced thousands of people to leave their homes.

treaties between American Indian tribes and the United States

Indian Removal Act

Before 1830, many tribes were considered **independent** nations. They had rights to their land. They made their own laws. But, settlers wanted to live on this land, and states wanted tribes to follow state laws.

In 1830, the **federal** government passed the Indian Removal Act. President Andrew Jackson thought the act was a good idea. He believed it would keep settlers and tribes from fighting. He thought it would help the United States grow. One of his predictions was right. The other was not.

The act gave the president power to **negotiate** treaties. Jackson told Eastern tribes to give up their lands and move west. The government reserved land in what is now Oklahoma for the tribes.

President Andrew Jackson

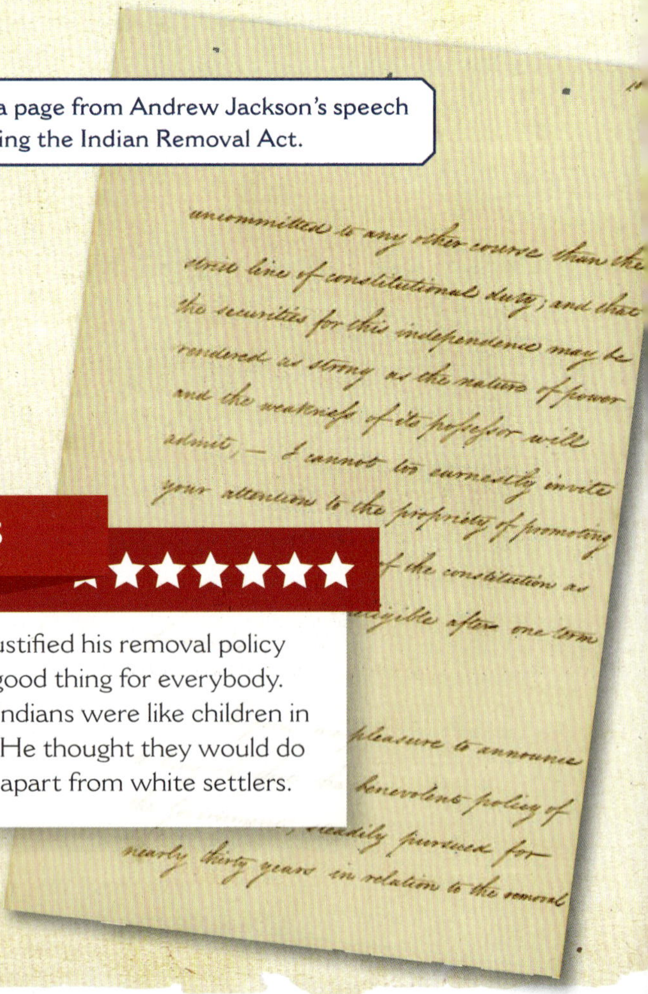

uncommitted to any other course than the
strict line of constitutional duty; and that
the securities for this independence may be
rendered as strong as the nature of power
and the weakness of its possessor will
admit, — I cannot too earnestly invite
your attention to the propriety of promoting
f the constitution as
eligible after one term
pleasure to announce
benevolent policy of
steadily pursued for
nearly thirty years in relation to the removal

This is a page from Andrew Jackson's speech explaining the Indian Removal Act.

JACKSON'S VIEWS

Andrew Jackson justified his removal policy by saying it was a good thing for everybody. He felt American Indians were like children in need of guidance. He thought they would do better if they lived apart from white settlers.

Removal was supposed to be voluntary and peaceful. American Indians who wished to stay on their land would need to give up their right to govern themselves and live like white people. But, most did not really have a choice. If tribes refused to move, Jackson used force. By 1837, the United States uprooted nearly all of the tribes east of the Mississippi River. Over 46,000 American Indians were forced to leave their homes. They had lived in the East for thousands of years. Now, they had to start over.

American Indians are forced to move west.

CROCKETT DEFENDS TRIBES

Not everyone agreed with Jackson's policies. Frontiersman, folk hero, and U.S. representative, David Crockett, bitterly opposed the Indian Removal Act. Crockett spoke out against the unfair treatment of American Indian tribes.

Trail of Tears

The Cherokee did not want to leave their homes. They asked the **Supreme Court** to recognize them as an independent nation with their own laws. In 1832, the Court agreed. But, President Jackson did not. He ordered the removal of the Cherokee people.

In 1835, a group of about 100 Cherokee members signed the Treaty of New Echota. In the treaty, they gave up claims to Eastern land. In exchange, they received land in Indian Territory, money, livestock, and other items. But none of the signers were main tribal leaders. Over 15,000 Cherokee signed a petition in protest. Jackson and many others ignored their complaint.

In 1838, U.S. troops drove the Cherokee from their homes. They forced them to walk over 1,200 miles (1,900 kilometers). Many suffered from hunger, cold, disease, and exhaustion. Over 4,000 died. After 116 days, the survivors reached Indian Territory. Their march is called the Trail of Tears because so many people died. The Cherokees call it the Place Where We Cried.

The Cherokee struggled in their new home. They had lived in villages and grew crops. Tribes on the Great Plains hunted buffalo. The government also sent tribes who were enemies to share the same land. It was a time of great sadness and hardship for many tribes.

JOHN ROSS

John Ross was a principal chief of the Cherokee nation. He spoke out against removal. In 1836, he told the U.S. government, "Our cause is your own. It is the cause of liberty and justice."

The Cherokee walk the Trail of Tears.

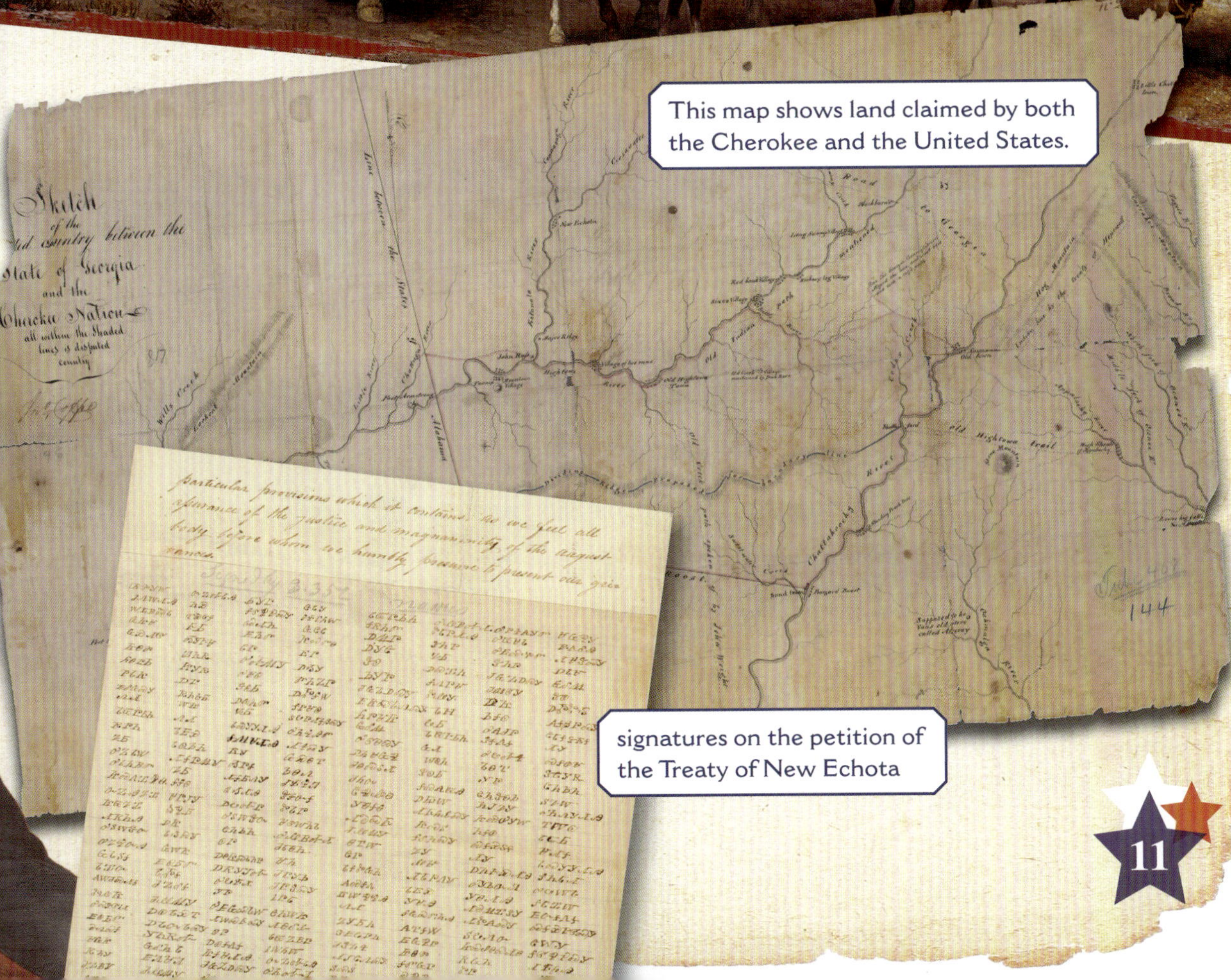

This map shows land claimed by both the Cherokee and the United States.

signatures on the petition of the Treaty of New Echota

Resistance

Some tribes refused to leave without a fight. Though often outnumbered, they defended their land and their rights.

The Seminole Wars

The Seminoles call themselves "free people." They have lived in Florida for hundreds of years. They welcomed people who escaped slavery and fought those who tried to take their lands. This angered the U.S. government. In 1817, the First Seminole War began. Andrew Jackson was a general at the time. He led a series of attacks on the tribe. After three months of fighting, many Seminoles were forced to leave their lands.

After the Indian Removal Act was signed, the government told the remaining Seminoles to move west. They refused. In 1835, the Second Seminole War began. It was the bloodiest war ever fought between a tribe and the U.S. Army. Fewer than 3,000 Seminoles fought more than 30,000 U.S. troops. In 1842, the Seminoles **surrendered**. They were forced to leave their land.

OSCEOLA

Osceola was a Seminole leader who led warriors during the Second Seminole War. In 1837, he agreed to discuss peace. But, the government tricked him and put him in prison, where he died three months later.

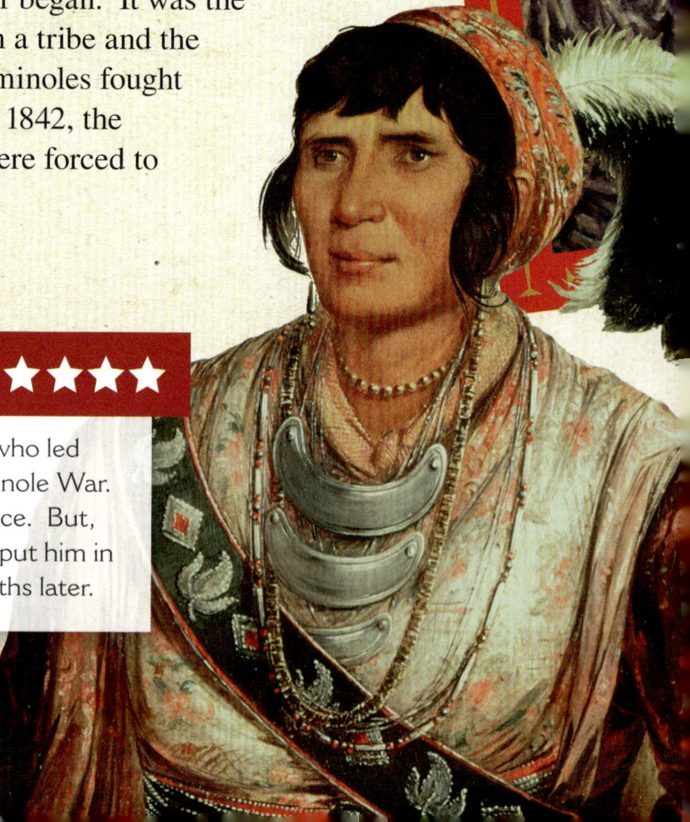

Seminoles attack a U.S. supply wagon in 1812.

A small group of Seminoles stayed behind. In 1855, the U.S. Army destroyed Seminole land in a final attempt to get the tribe to move west. So, the Seminoles attacked a nearby military camp. This began the Third Seminole War. Small fights took place over two years until Seminole leader Billy Bowlegs surrendered for his people.

The removal of the Seminoles cost many lives. Sadly, it was not the only time blood was shed for tribal land.

Red Cloud's War

When gold was discovered in Montana, miners rushed to seek their fortunes. They followed an ancient trail the Lakota used to hunt buffalo. The route became known as the Bozeman Trail. The U.S. Army built roads and forts along the trail. This violated the First Treaty of Fort Laramie. The Lakota fiercely resisted the **invasion** of their lands.

Red Cloud was a Lakota war chief. He fought to protect his homeland. In 1866, he led one of the most successful wars against the U.S. Army ever fought by an American Indian tribe. His men attacked U.S. workers along the Bozeman Trail. The attacks were successful. In 1868, the United States recognized the Lakota's rights to the land with the Second Treaty of Fort Laramie.

KILLING BUFFALO

Tribes of the Plains relied on the buffalo for survival. The American government encouraged hunters to kill the buffalo. In just a few years, they killed millions of buffalo.

Red Cloud put down his weapons. But, he continued to stand up for the rights of his people until his death in 1909. He even traveled to Washington, DC, to talk with U.S. leaders.

Many of Red Cloud's followers kept fighting. In 1874, gold was discovered in the Black Hills. The Lakota again fought to defend their land.

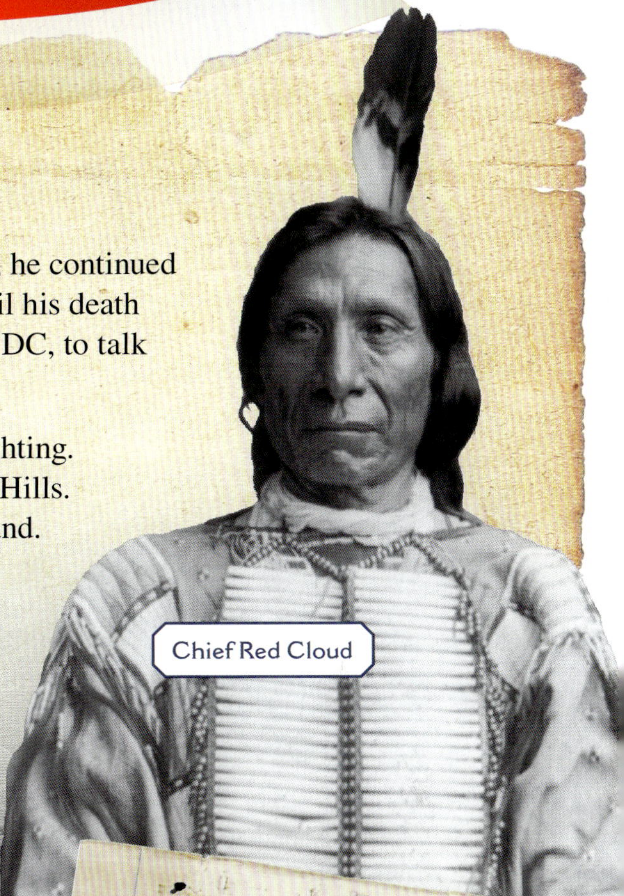

Chief Red Cloud

American Indians battle U.S. forces during Red Cloud's War.

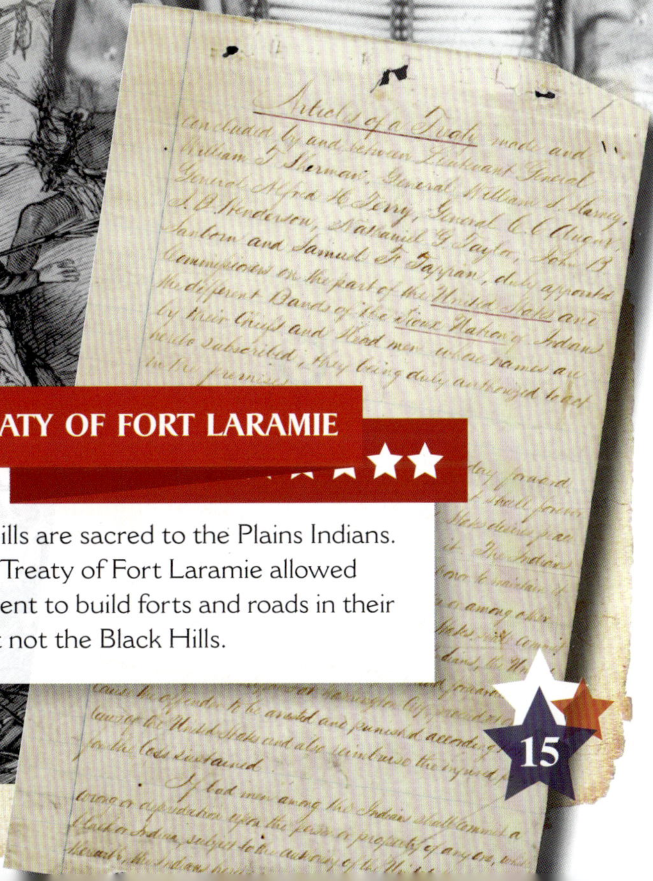

Articles of a Treaty made and concluded by and between Lieutenant General William T. Sherman, General William S. Harney, General Alfred H. Terry, General C. C. Augur, J. B. Henderson, Nathaniel G. Taylor, John B. Sanborn and Samuel F. Tappan, duly appointed commissioners on the part of the United States and the different Bands of the Sioux Nation of Indians by their Chiefs and Head men whose names are hereto subscribed, they being duly authorized to act in the premises.

SECOND TREATY OF FORT LARAMIE

The Black Hills are sacred to the Plains Indians. The Second Treaty of Fort Laramie allowed the government to build forts and roads in their territory, but not the Black Hills.

The Battle of the Little Bighorn

In 1874, George Armstrong Custer led U.S. troops onto Lakota lands. They found gold in the Black Hills. When the news got out, gold fever spread quickly. Miners and settlers poured into Lakota land. The government tried to buy the Black Hills, but the Lakota refused to sell.

So, the government ignored the Second Treaty of Fort Laramie. U.S. leaders ordered the Lakota to move to a **reservation**. They refused to leave. On June 25, 1876, Custer and his troops tried to force them out. They found Lakota Chief Sitting Bull and over 2,000 warriors camped near the Little Bighorn River. Custer and his men attacked. He made a disastrous decision when he split his men into three groups. The separate groups were not able to help each other. Cut off by the tribes, Custer and all 210 of his soldiers were killed. The battle became known as Custer's Last Stand.

This victory showed the great strength of the tribes. It also enraged white settlers. Federal troops flooded the area. They drove the people of the Plains onto reservations. This ended their way of life.

George Armstrong Custer

Custer's last stand

CRAZY HORSE

Crazy Horse led a group of Lakota Indians called the Oglala. His warriors won many battles against U.S. troops. He and his warriors helped defeat Custer at the Battle of the Little Bighorn.

The Nez Percé attack white settlers.

Nez Percé warriors

The Nez Percé War

The Nez Percé (PUHRS) lived in parts of what are now Idaho, Oregon, and Washington. The United States recognized their land in an 1855 treaty. But miners found gold there in 1860. Miners and settlers rushed to the area in hopes of striking it rich. So, the government wrote a new treaty. The new treaty took land from the Nez Percé. Most of the tribe refused to sign. They called it the "Thief Treaty." Still, they were told to leave.

Several young warriors were angry at being forced from their home. They killed many white settlers. The tribe's leader, Chief Joseph, thought federal troops would seek revenge. In June 1877, he and his people chose to flee to safety in Canada.

The Nez Percé walked across 1,300 mi. (2,400 km) of rough land. Their group included only 250 warriors. Yet, about 5,000 U.S. troops followed them. They fought many times along the way. The Nez Percé won nearly every skirmish. It was a brilliant military **retreat**. But their weapons were no match for the troops. The Nez Percé surrendered on October 5, 1877. They were only 40 mi. (64 km) from the Canadian border.

This war ended many years of fighting between the people of the Plains and the U.S. Army. By this point, nearly all the tribes had surrendered their freedom for reservation life.

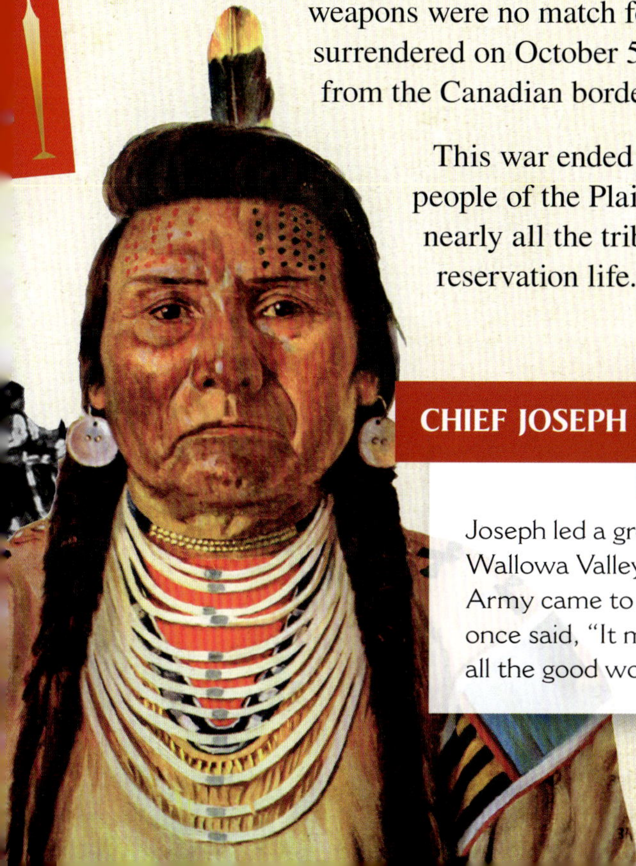

CHIEF JOSEPH

Joseph led a group of Nez Percé in eastern Oregon's Wallowa Valley. He valued peace, but when the U.S. Army came to his home, he protected his people. He once said, "It makes my heart sick when I remember all the good words and all the broken promises."

Wounded Knee

Plains Indians on reservations faced hunger, disease, and broken promises. Many turned to Wovoka, a Paiute (PI-yoot) **prophet.** He promised that if they performed the Ghost Dance, the people and buffalo killed by settlers would return. He also said the dance would make the settlers disappear. This frightened settlers who thought the tribes would attack.

Plains Indians perform the Ghost Dance.

SITTING BULL

Sitting Bull was a Lakota chief who was at the Battle of the Little Bighorn. He organized the Plains tribes against the U.S. Army. He is remembered for his fierce resistance to government control.

the massacre at Wounded Knee

Chief Sitting Bull never performed the Ghost Dance himself. But, he encouraged others to dance and he resisted white authority. The government feared he would leave the reservation. In 1890, tribal police came to arrest him. During the arrest, Sitting Bull was killed. Other Lakota fled the reservation. Troops rounded them up and ordered them to encamp on Wounded Knee Creek.

The next day, soldiers tried to take the Lakota Indians' weapons. An argument broke out over one man's rifle. A shot was fired and a soldier fell. The troops then fired at the American Indians from close range. Troops hunted down those who fled. Some were killed miles from the camp. More than 200 Lakota men, women, and children were **massacred** (MAH-suh-kerd).

Sitting Bull's death and the massacre at Wounded Knee marked the end of resistance on the Great Plains. For American Indians, Wounded Knee is a powerful symbol. It represents the unfair treatment by the U.S. government and the loss of their way of life.

Resilience

By the end of the 19th century, most tribes lived on reservations. The United States defined these lands through treaties. At first, American Indians were not allowed to leave the reservations for any reason. They had a hard time finding jobs. They depended on the government to meet their needs.

Today, hundreds of reservations cover millions of acres of land. Most are in rural areas. This means they are not near cities. Reservations are very different from each other. Some have plenty of natural resources and land that is easy to farm. Others do not. Some reservations are huge. The Navajo Reservation is the largest. It covers about 16 million acres, about the size of present-day West Virginia. Other reservations are very small. The smallest is less than 100 acres, about the size of a small farm.

Reservations are like small nations. They have their own governments. Most tribes have a **constitution**. People elect their own leaders and councils. They manage their lands, pass laws, and collect taxes. They have their own courts, too.

Today, American Indians are free to live anywhere they choose. Many now live away from their reservations. But some come back to visit. They spend time with their families. They take part in tribal events. Reservations help American Indians stay connected with their past while looking toward the future.

Lakota reservation in 1891

a reservation today

"ASSIMILATION"

The United States tried to change American Indian **cultures** through a process called "assimilation." In the 1800s, children were separated from their families and sent to boarding schools to prevent them from learning about their tribes' cultures.

For many years, tribal leaders traveled to Washington, DC, to remind the U.S. government of the promises made in treaties. They took their cases to the Supreme Court. The Court ruled in many cases that the treaties were still valid. This was a huge step for many tribes.

Tribes also fought for recognition. When a tribe has federal recognition, it is accepted as an independent nation. This means members of the tribe make the decisions. They have their own governments and make their own laws. It also gives them access to federal programs and protection. This can be achieved through treaties and court decisions. Today, there are more than 565 federally recognized tribes.

American Indians showed **resilience** in the face of great suffering. They had their homes taken away from them. They were forced to walk thousands of miles. Settlers mined for gold and took their land. They fought with soldiers many times to protect their rights. Today, tribes remember their histories. They continue to fight for their rights as they look to the future.

Laws are discussed at the Navajo Nation Council Chamber.

American Indians march in a parade in Montana.

Looking Ahead

Many American Indians today live just like other Americans. They are our friends, neighbors, and classmates. They live in all kinds of houses and shop at the same stores as other people. They also celebrate their cultures. They share their ways with others. Americans are starting to understand all the contributions tribes have made to the country.

There is still important work to do. **Stereotypes** paint an inaccurate picture of American Indians. They show American Indians living in tepees and dressed in feathers. Some sports mascots and team names also reflect a negative view of American Indians. The truth is much more complex and interesting. It is part of a story that all of us should know. It is part of our story. Understanding American Indian perspectives helps us understand our nation.

Americans today must learn from the past so we can grow stronger as a country. We should respect those who were here first. Our world is full of people who walk different paths. We have different ways of life. We need to celebrate this **diversity** and learn to walk side by side.

an American Indian family

a school on the Navajo reservation

PRESERVING HISTORY

The National Museum of the American Indian works to share the lives, languages, and cultures of tribes across the Americas. The museum collects and stores objects that tell the history of each tribe.

the National Museum of the American Indian in Washington, DC

Remember It!

A monument is a structure that honors a person or an event from the past. A monument can be a sculpture, a statue, a fountain, or even an entire park.

Design a monument for a person or an event from this book. Think about how you want people to remember the person or event you chose. How do you want them to feel when they see it? Create your design using whatever materials you feel are best. You can even go digital! Then, share your design with your class.

Crazy Horse Memorial in South Dakota

headstones from the Battle of the Little Bighorn

Glossary

constitution—a system of beliefs, laws, and principles by which a country or state is governed

cultures—the beliefs and ways of groups of people

diversity—being made up of characteristics that are different from each other

endure—to continue to exist in the same way

federal—relating to the main government of the United States

frontier—an area where few people live

independent—not controlled or ruled by another country

inevitable—something that is impossible to avoid or that is sure to happen

invasion—the act of entering a place to try to take control of it

massacred—violently killed many people

native—belonging to a person or group of people from birth or childhood

negotiate—formally discuss something in order to make an agreement

prophet—a person who says or foretells what will happen in the future

reservation—land set aside especially for American Indians to live and work

resilience—the ability to become strong and successful again after something bad happens

retreat—a military strategy that involves pulling back or leaving a battle

stereotypes—unfair beliefs that all the people in a group are the same

Supreme Court—the highest court of law in the United States

surrendered—agreed to stop fighting because you knew you would not win

treaties—formal agreements that are made between two or more countries or groups

unavailing—not useful

Index

Black Hills, 15–16

buffalo, 10, 14, 20

Cherokee, 10–11

Chief Joseph, 19

Crazy Horse, 17, 28

Crockett, David, 9

Custer, George Armstrong, 16–17

Everett, Edward, 4

Fort Laramie, First Treaty of, 14

Fort Laramie, Second Treaty of, 14–16

Ghost Dance, 20–21

Great Britain, 5

Great Plains, 10, 14–16, 19–21

Indian Removal Act, 8–9, 12, 32

Indian Territory, 10

Jackson, Andrew, 8–10, 12, 32

Lakota, 14–17, 20–22

Little Bighorn, Battle of the, 16–17, 20, 29

New Echota, Treaty of, 10–11

Nez Percé, 18–19

Osceola, 12

Red Cloud's War, 14–15

reservation, 16, 19–23, 27

Ross, John, 10

Seminoles, 12–13

Sitting Bull, 16, 20–21

Trail of Tears, 10–11

Wounded Knee, 20–21

Your Turn!

uncommitted to any other course than the strict line of constitutional duty; and that the securities for this independence may be rendered as strong as the nature of power and the weakness of its possessor will admit, — I cannot too earnestly invite your attention to the propriety of promoting such an amendment of the constitution as will render him ineligible after one term of service.

It gives me pleasure to announce to Congress that the benevolent policy of the Government, steadily pursued for nearly thirty years in relation to the removal

Let Them Stay!

The U.S. government forced American Indians to leave their homes when it passed the Indian Removal Act in 1830. In this speech, President Jackson speaks out in favor of removing American Indians from their homelands. Write a letter to Jackson explaining why this act is unfair. Propose a better solution to the problem.